NORTH AMERICAN ANIMALS

Diamondback Rattlesnakes

by Betsy Rathburn

BLASTOFF! READERS
3

BELLWETHER MEDIA • MINNEAPOLIS, MN

Note to Librarians, Teachers, and Parents:

Blastoff! Readers are carefully developed by literacy experts and combine standards-based content with developmentally appropriate text.

Level 1 provides the most support through repetition of high-frequency words, light text, predictable sentence patterns, and strong visual support.

Level 2 offers early readers a bit more challenge through varied simple sentences, increased text load, and less repetition of high-frequency words.

Level 3 advances early-fluent readers toward fluency through increased text and concept load, less reliance on visuals, longer sentences, and more literary language.

Level 4 builds reading stamina by providing more text per page, increased use of punctuation, greater variation in sentence patterns, and increasingly challenging vocabulary.

Level 5 encourages children to move from "learning to read" to "reading to learn" by providing even more text, varied writing styles, and less familiar topics.

Whichever book is right for your reader, Blastoff! Readers are the perfect books to build confidence and encourage a love of reading that will last a lifetime!

This edition first published in 2018 by Bellwether Media, Inc.

No part of this publication may be reproduced in whole or in part without written permission of the publisher. For information regarding permission, write to Bellwether Media, Inc., Attention: Permissions Department, 5357 Penn Avenue South, Minneapolis, MN 55419.

Library of Congress Cataloging-in-Publication Data

Names: Rathburn, Betsy, author.
Title: Diamondback Rattlesnakes / by Betsy Rathburn.
Description: Minneapolis, MN : Bellwether Media, Inc., [2018] | Series:
   Blastoff! Readers: North American Animals | Audience: Age 5-8. | Audience:
   K to grade 3. | Includes bibliographical references and index.
Identifiers: LCCN 2016054956 (print) | LCCN 2017005261 (ebook) | ISBN
   9781626176379 (hardcover : alk. paper) | ISBN 9781681033679 (ebook)
Subjects: LCSH: Eastern diamondback rattlesnake–Juvenile literature. |
   Western diamondback rattlesnake–Juvenile literature.
Classification: LCC QL666.O69 R37 2018 (print) | LCC QL666.O69 (ebook) | DDC
   597.96/38–dc23
LC record available at https://lccn.loc.gov/2016054956

Editor: Nathan Sommer   Designer: Josh Brink

Printed in the United States of America, North Mankato, MN

Table of Contents

What Are Diamondback Rattlesnakes?

rattle

western diamondback

Diamondback rattlesnakes are **reptiles** known for their noisy **rattles**. A bold diamond pattern covers their bodies.

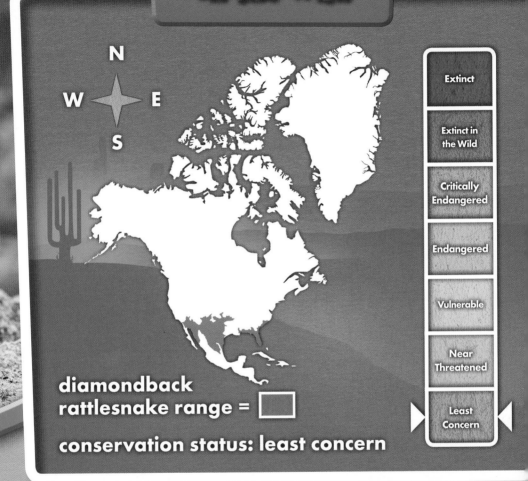

N
W E
S

Extinct

Extinct in the Wild

Critically Endangered

Endangered

Vulnerable

Near Threatened

Least Concern

diamondback rattlesnake range = ☐

conservation status: least concern

Western diamondbacks are found in the southwestern United States and northern Mexico. Eastern diamondbacks live in the southeastern United States.

Diamondbacks live in dry **habitats**. They sneak around deserts, grasslands, and mountains.

Diamondbacks often hide during the day. They find shelter in tree stumps, rock piles, and animal **burrows**.

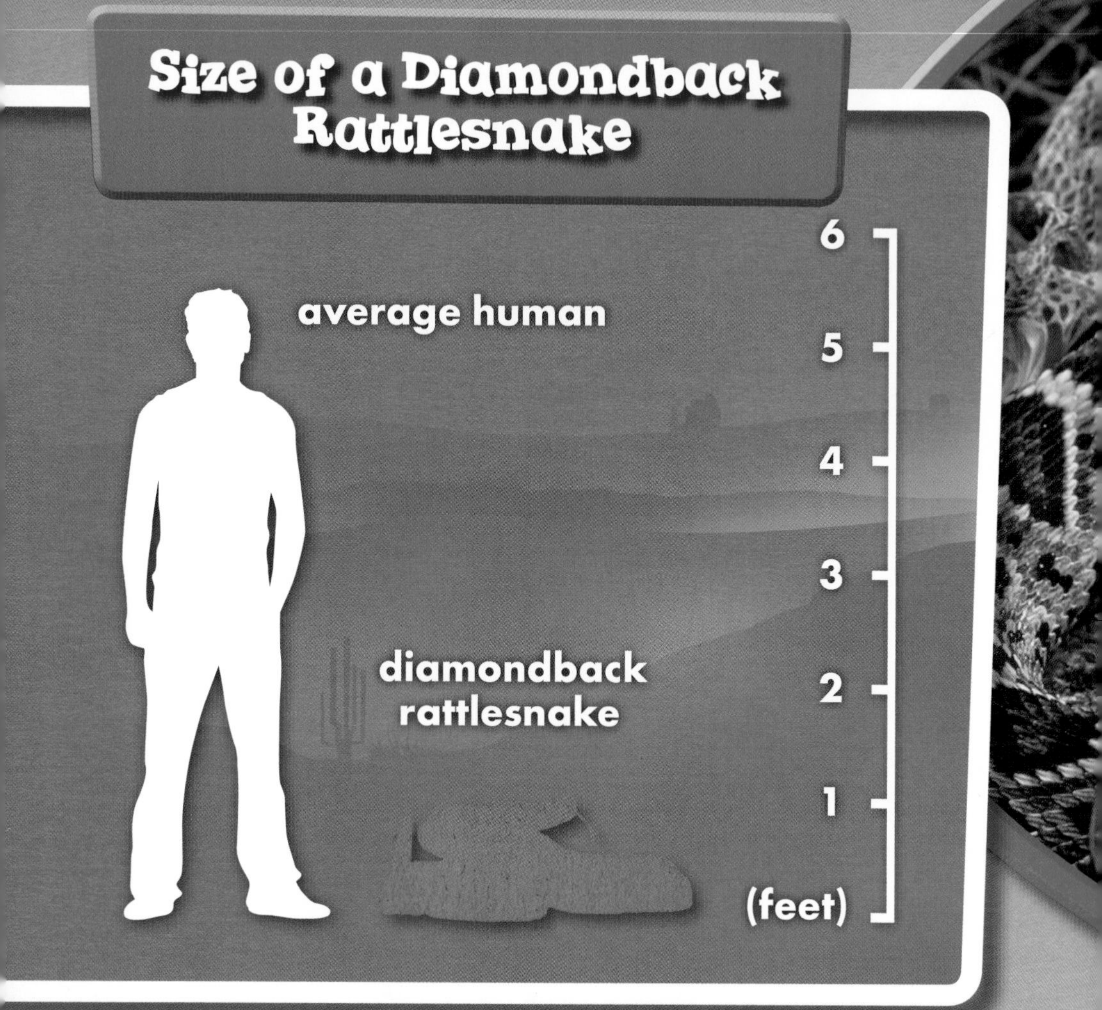

Size of a Diamondback Rattlesnake

average human

diamondback
rattlesnake

6

5

4

3

2

1

(feet)

Diamondbacks are some of the longest rattlesnakes in North America. They can grow up to 8 feet (2.4 meters) long.

skin

eastern
diamondback

The snakes shed their skin as they grow. The last **scales** on their tails become part of their rattles!

Diamondbacks are **carnivores**. They eat mice and other small animals.

Gambel's quails

gray squirrels

pocket mice

cottontail rabbits

northern mockingbirds

spiny lizards

Most diamondbacks eat once every few weeks. They open their jaws wide to swallow **prey** whole.

These snakes hide until food is near. At night, **pits** near their eyes help them sense the heat of other animals.

pit

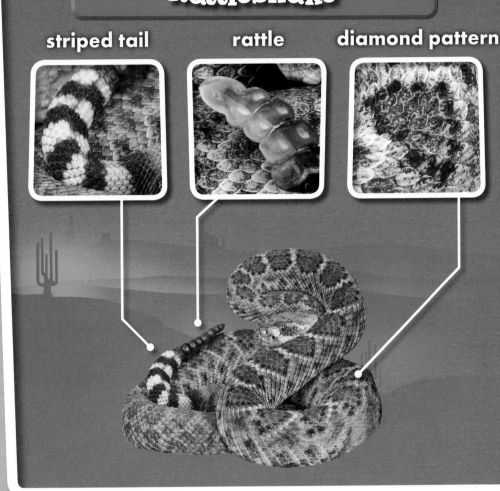

Identify a Diamondback Rattlesnake

striped tail

rattle

diamond pattern

When prey comes close, diamondbacks strike! Sharp **fangs** shoot deadly **venom** into the animals.

13

Diamondbacks must watch out for enemies. Horses and deer stomp on the snakes if they come too close.

deer

red-tailed
hawks

roadrunners

eastern
kingsnakes

Birds of prey catch them
with sharp claws and beaks.
Sometimes, other snakes will
even snack on diamondbacks!

Diamondbacks rattle their tails when they sense danger. They curl into tight **coils** and raise their heads in warning.

The biggest diamondbacks can strike enemies from over 5 feet (1.5 meters) away!

Some diamondbacks **hibernate** in winter. They stay hidden until spring.

Females usually have babies during the summer. The babies grow in eggs inside mom. Then the mom gives birth to live babies.

button tail

Newborn diamondbacks are up to 15 inches (38 centimeters) long. They are born with button tails and sharp fangs. Soon, the babies leave mom. They **slither** off to hunt for food!

Baby Facts

Name for babies:	neonates
Size of litter:	6 to 21
Time spent inside egg:	5 to 7 months
Time spent with mom:	1 day

Glossary

burrows—holes or tunnels that some animals dig for homes

carnivores—animals that only eat meat

coils—series of loops

fangs—sharp, hollow teeth; venom flows through fangs and into a bite.

habitats—lands with certain types of plants, animals, and weather

hibernate—to spend the winter sleeping or resting

pits—heat-sensing holes around the mouth; diamondback rattlesnakes use pits to hunt for food at night.

prey—animals that are hunted by other animals for food

rattles—groups of hard, loose scales that cover the ends of rattlesnake tails

reptiles—cold-blooded animals that have backbones and lay eggs

scales—small plates of skin that cover and protect a rattlesnake's body

slither—to move by smoothly sliding back and forth

venom—poison created by diamondback rattlesnakes

To Learn More

AT THE LIBRARY
Bowman, Chris. *Western Diamondback Rattlesnakes.* Minneapolis, Minn.: Bellwether Media, 2014.

McFadden, Jesse. *Watch Out for Rattlesnakes!* New York, N.Y.: PowerKids Press, 2016.

Statts, Leo. *Rattlesnakes.* Minneapolis, Minn.: Abdo Zoom, 2017.

ON THE WEB
Learning more about diamondback rattlesnakes is as easy as 1, 2, 3.

1. Go to www.factsurfer.com.

2. Enter "diamondback rattlesnakes" into the search box.

3. Click the "Surf" button and you will see a list of related web sites.

With factsurfer.com, finding more information is just a click away.

Index

The images in this book are reproduced through the courtesy of: lokvi, front cover; Ryan M. Bolton, p. 4; Johnaudrey, p. 6; Bill Gorum/ Alamy, p. 7; Mc Donald Wildlife Ph/ age fotostock, p. 9; David Welling/ Nature Picture Library, p. 10; vagabond54, p. 11 (top left); IrinaK, p. 11 (top right); Charles A. Drost and Jan Hart/ Wiki Commons, p. 11 (center left); Maria Jeffs, p. 11 (center right); Michael J Thompson, p. 11 (bottom left); Vladimir Wrangel, p. 11 (bottom right); Audrey Snider-Bell, pp. 12, 13 (top left, top center, top right, bottom); John Cancalosi/ Getty Images, p. 14; JAMES PIERCE, p. 15 (top left); Le Do, p. 15 (top right); Jason Mintzer, p. 15 (bottom left); fivespots, p. 15 (bottom right); franzfoto.com/ Alamy, p. 16; Jim Zipp/ age fotostock, p. 17; Zigmund Leszczynski/ age fotostock, pp. 18-19; Paul & Joyce Berquist, p. 20; Iulian Gherghel, p. 21.